Maxims

Serge DuGarbandier

Published by Conscious Publishing, 2025.

While every precaution has been taken in the preparation of this book, the publisher assumes no responsibility for errors or omissions, or for damages resulting from the use of the information contained herein.

MAXIMS

First edition. June 24, 2025.

Copyright © 2025 Serge DuGarbandier.

ISBN: 978-1929096220

Written by Serge DuGarbandier.

Translated by Felicity Troux.

Cover: Texas Red, *Voletic Waves 18,* 2024.

There are only two things. Truth and lies.

Truth is indivisible, hence it cannot recognize itself;

anyone who wants to recognize it has to be a lie.

Franz Kafka

There must be a reason for the universe, or the irrational would make no sense.

If the world were governed by chance, it would be much more orderly than it is.

To say what lies beyond reason would be like judging without judging or washing the fur without wetting it.

The misfortune of always loving where we are not loved is only a symptom of the malady of never loving where we are.

Virtue is indeed its own reward. In this respect it resembles justice conceived as pure revenge.

Socrates, famous for his irony, is also famous for the doctrine that virtue is knowledge.

Justice is a necessary evil. It's a pity everyone's so keen on it.

2

Alice concludes from the Jabberwocky poem that somebody must have killed something. With this she sums up not only epic poetry, but all of myth.

The most important numbers are not just irrational but transcendental. They're not proper numbers at all, but relations.

The imaginary numbers turn quantity into quality, arithmetic into geometry. Love is imaginary – fictitious, if you must – in much the same way.

It's not love or money, but jealousy that turns the world.

Without jealousy, no obscenity.

The garden path of falsehood by no means leads into a wilderness, but rather up to a house of considerable architectural interest.

Those who have never experienced tragedy understand life only in theory – close kin, as Kant saw, to comedy.

Some people smile after almost everything they say, like an animal baring its teeth.

Our lives are organized around lies and concealments superimposed upon ancient errors. Once the cover-up has been achieved, it's no more possible to undo it than to take off your clothes and go naked.

Our words are like the leeches employed by old physicians. In bleeding their patients, they profess to cure them.

Erotic love is an incomplete synesthesia in which people generally smell and taste as they look but feel as they sound.

It's clear that what is false is generally clearer than what is true.

Logic alone has the beauty of real wilderness; sentiment likes gardens, however wild they may appear.

One must lie to people to avoid deceiving them by telling the truth.

4

Brian Rotman's attempt to conceive a finite mathematics is wonderfully Quixotic, although more suited to a tipsy Sancho Pansa.

Thought must play, otherwise it wouldn't work.

Rien means nothing in the sense of bugger all, whereas *le néant* has a definite article and means nothingness. The distance between them is the perineum between what gives birth and what does not. Twin holes - and all the vacuums of space - are filled with virtual particles.

Not all maxims need be true, but a few must be.

Unhappy love attracts almost everybody but its object.

One of the surest ways to attract someone is to be passionately in love with someone else.

True maxims are unlikely to yield much pleasure, as La Rochefoucauld observed, unless we think ourselves superior to them.

I once met a man at a party who had loved three sets of twins, and in each case began with one but ended with her sister. This recalls the problem faced by someone choosing between two bags one of which has twice as much money as the other. If you choose the bag with $x, say, you should really have chosen the other one, since the probable value of choosing it is ½(2x) + ½(x/2) =1.25x. The twins don't even need to be identical.

Was it by way of endearing expiation, after his mental collapse, that John Nash confessed that he had overestimated human rationality? For game theory has nothing to say about human beings - except of course that they produced it.

Nature has a mania for symmetry.

Depending on the faces of their owners, specular bums appear as either ducks or rabbits.

To turn on a bicycle we must turn the handlebars slightly the wrong way first.

Honesty is by no means to be confused with truthfulness.

6

I heard that if homeless people told the truth no one would believe them. As far as that goes, we're all homeless.

Some animals lie better than us, not least by persuading us that they are incapable of it. There was a keeper who rowed a monkey to a little island on an English baronial estate, because monkeys, as you know, don't like to swim except in emergencies. Getting out of his boat, he turned his head to see the monkey rowing back to shore. Did I dream this? Not at all.

How tendentious to go on proclaiming that humans are animals. So what? More interesting are the animals that wouldn't exist without us, and who imitate us so well - like Clever Hans.

We have very little idea of how animals do almost anything. Consider the nightingale, let alone a murder of crows.

Absolute chagrin remakes the world.

There's no better guide to our values than our swear words.

Since the Enlightenment, blasphemy has given way to obscenity: God and Hell to Bugger and Shit.

By far the holiest word in modern America is *cunt*. Despite everything, New York is still a long way from Paris - where *con* is so common as to mean virtually nothing.

The whole point of music is to fuck it up.

Beauty spots [*grains de beauté*] demonstrate how its violation is fundamental to beauty. Artificial moles were all the rage in the Enlightenment.

The feminist thrust of comedy has traditionally been symbolized not by the vagina, but the anus - egalitarian as it is. The music is played on wind instruments even in the tragedy of *Othello*.

The anus is a puncture on the patriarchal bicycle. It can no more be mended by a doctor than by a repair outfit. The police accordingly resort to desperate measures.

Bataille was rhapsodic about what he coyly called *le petit*; but it took an Irishman to structure an entire book around it.

Division by zero is axiomatic in Shakespeare. *A Midsummer Night's Dream* is full of amusing arithmetic, but at the bottom of it all is Bottom: the obscene O.

Boolean algebra and Russell's paradox prove the logic of exclusion to be more fundamental than that of identity.

One is double-faced because one has two contraries: many and none.

One is forced to begin with something or nothing. European mathematics found solid ground in Euclidean geometry but was swept off its feet by the Indian zero and has never fully recovered.

One is now defined as the empty set, as though it were Buddhist.

Love means nothing in tennis, and in *Much Ado About Nothing* it's like being tickled to death with a holy thistle.

Our great Voltaire found the *cul-de-sac* too vulgar, so no wonder Shakespeare was a complete impasse to him.

The ideal maxim is like a mathematical point. Ideal reading is a sort of projective geometry.

Misconstruing emptiness is disastrous for the less intelligent (Nagarjuna).

***

Maxims lie halfway between art and thought; hence their traditional domain is virtue.

Moralistic people are fatal to morality. They make criminals seem authentic.

Morality is the death duty on beauty. "Love is too young to know what conscience is…"

After the sense of pain, the sense of sight is most coercive. Utopias are peopled by the blind.

We generally act as we think we look.

Our view of others is a function of how much they resemble us. *Honi soit qui mal y pense.*

That poetry aspires to music is a dubious maxim.

Tunes can be transposed in key, but there is no analogue for colors. Music is objectively relative, whereas painting is subjectively absolute. That's why perfect pitch is compared to color recognition.

Abstract painting exists only in theory, as a model of what art would be if it were science. But to a certain extent all painting is abstract.

Music is not a universal language, though naturally it tries to be and says it is.

Music depends on discord even more than harmony. It began not just as an accompaniment to war but as a weapon, and its origins were never very far from the Brazen Bull.

Music without words was regarded as dangerous not only by medieval Christians but by Enlightenment atheists. Tolstoy's "Kreutzer Sonata" is the *reductio ad absurdum* of the crusade, as though Beethoven were responsible for the author's own infidelities.

The overture to *Don Giovanni* is by far the most erotic part.

Good and evil are often identical in form. The trap is the mirror.

Laughter both presupposes and produces tears.

Considered as politics, charity offends justice even more than crime.

In loving as many people as possible, the libertine resembles the saint. What sets them apart isn't so much their kind of love as the nature of the possible.

There are both libertine and Augustinian views of La Rochefoucauld – not surprising, as the saint was himself a libertine.

Erotic love is an orthodox image of the sacred even in the Bible. The *sacrum* is a pelvic bone.

I forget which Pope made women go naked on all fours after chestnuts. Probably the same one who was tried after his death, had his body exhumed and its blessing fingers amputated, but was later reinterred in the Christian cemetery.

Love both dotes and antidotes.

If you want to find religion, look in the heart of an atheist. (Baudelaire)

So-called "Woke" morality emerges quite logically in America from the backside and tail end of Christian culture - where the victim *par excellence* is God.

Virtue was first masculine, then feminine, and finally neutered - like *das Mädchen*.

The priest has been poisoned by the doctor; virtue circumcised by health.

We generally prevaricate between diagnoses of illness and evil just as it suits us.

14

Mental illnesses are figural diseases, like Nabokov's "referential mania."

Kafka's only story about sex ends with the doctor in bed with the patient. Take note.

Where love's the case, the doctor's an ass.

Transference is one of the few facts of psychoanalysis. It goes both ways - as when Anaïs Nin fucked Otto Rank.

Clever doctors, like shamans, imitate their patients.

Obsession, considered a disease, is really the mind trying to cure itself by repetition that little by little transforms the original.

It is often observed, but not often enough, that we wash too much for our own health.

Freedom of religion is a contradiction at the heart of every democracy.

Critics of religion make the same mistake as its adherents, taking its dogmas at once too literally and not literally enough.

The word is made flesh every day - if not in church or bed, then in the pharmacy.

The rich and poor share a proclivity to drug addiction. Life's either too hard or too easy.

Having absurdly persecuted marijuana for decades, we now tout its medical benefits while proposing in almost the same breath to criminalize tobacco, or at any rate to make cigarettes so dear as to ruin those who certainly have the most right to smoke them. Have we forgotten how we used to give tobacco to our soldiers, and how even butt ends were worth more than gold in Auschwitz?

Those who fantasize about a future in which medicine triumphs over death seem not to realize that they're dreaming of the absolutization of murder. Or perhaps that's the dream.

16

The American practice of attempting to cure prisoners who have gone mad on death row – so as to execute them – reveals a basic principle of modern law.

Not only have we quite often made death the penalty for attempted suicide, but we've even hanged the dead. What a species!

Capital punishment should be made voluntary.

That suicide is favored by the elderly and adolescents is an indictment of middle-age.

The seventeenth-century debate over whether babies could be baptized by holy water squirted up the vagina is the same bloody one we're still engaged in.

The only people free of prejudice against the old are young children. Everyone else is just pretending.

Those who devote themselves to social causes are often inept when it comes to individual suffering.

In the Middle Ages they made a distinction between mad and sane suicides, torturing only the latter. Now one can be locked up indefinitely for even considering the problem that Camus deemed essential to every philosophy.

That a divorce lawyer makes ten times more than a soldier on the front line makes all claims to a just society null and void.

Private virtue is infinitely preferable to public justice.

The distinction between public and private makes everything duplicitous.

One of Freud's more amusing dicta is that to dream of clothing means to dream of nakedness.

The sumptuary laws of modesty prohibited too much fancy clothing. Spartan men and women both competed naked. Why not ours?

18

The double-bind of modesty is that it's the basic mechanism of seduction.

Female underwear was at first fiercely resisted by moralists on the grounds that women shouldn't have anything between their legs. Now the thread between butt-cheeks is the last hurrah of modesty.

I recently read a choreographer for whom urinating on cue and half-undressed is more important to her sort of art than performing tedious old dance moves. The one thing to avoid, she says, is full nudity – unutterably dull.

When I last went to Berlin, respectable Berliners were still advertising for naked students to clean their houses. Imagine this at Harvard or the Sorbonne!

The tragicomedy of sexual reform is well illustrated by D.H Lawrence and Bertrand Russell who planned to set up a nudist colony in Central America. Strange bedfellows one may think – though they also shared Lady Ottoline Morrell.

The final goal of education is to arrive at something worth unlearning.

***

The greater part of philosophy is best regarded as a branch of satire.

Idealism and materialism are tautologies. Life is not one. You don't even live once.

Disillusioned people tend to conclude that everybody is self-interested. But it's much worse than that.

Modern aesthetics is enslaved by the idea of art. Kant was right to insist on the beauty of flowers – including, as his footnote says, their genitalia.

The old joke about Kant's cunt is vulgar but pertinent. He says that the human body cannot be a norm for beauty, but only an ideal. The norm is reserved for flowers.

It is impossible to say whether the flowers of philosophy are witty or beautiful. (Friedrich Schlegel)

What most annoyed Hegel about Schlegel was his dithyrambic fantasy with the woman on top. It's no accident that Humbert Humbert's two wives are compared to Schlegel and Hegel in *Lolita*.

The best thing about art galleries, as Bonnard said, is their windows.

To the joke about the philosophy student who fails an exam for looking out of the window should be added the one about the student who finds there is no window to look out of.

Iterating the natural numbers is like every day saying you're giving up smoking. Are you always doing the same thing or something different?

The relation between quantity and quality is poorly understood. "If n is not a number, then n itself is the only member of the series of natural numbers ending in n - if that is not too shocking a way of putting it." (Frege)

It is unwise to spend life indicting false premises, let alone those who treasure them.

Science defeats commonsense by refuting or revising it. Commonsense defeats science by pointing to things that can be neither revised nor refuted.

Socrates, like Nabokov, feared that ideas are the money of the mind.

Lovers of money are called materialists, but they're speculative idealists - like fetishists.

Fetishists view parts in the same way that more conventional people view holes.

According to Herodotus, Gyges - who invented money - was asked by the king to spy on the naked queen to confirm her beauty. Like the value of money, hers needed a second opinion - and that, of course, was the end of the king.

Inequality of wealth is dangerous when it gets out of hand, but desirable as a compensation for other causes of inequality, like being born ugly or stupid.

The rich usually think they're intelligent, and others follow suit.

The best short-term economic strategy is to bet on who will lose - on whole nations if necessary.

Despite appearances, philosophy and poetry are identical in their claim to differ. But they differ in reality as well as appearance, at least inasmuch as reality is determined by appearances.

Except in Plato, Western philosophers generally drink water, while the poets complain that water is far too strong and needs to be diluted. Plato was the greatest poet of Western philosophers. He never says anything, drunk or sober.

The opposition between art and science is not between subjective and objective, feeling and intellect, or old and new. There are simply two kinds of experiment: repeatable and not.

It's not truth that's fiction, but fiction.

The publisher's conventional disclaimer - *any resemblance to actual persons, living or dead, or actual events is purely coincidental* – is a lie worth pondering.

Absolute chance is the name of a necessary lie.

Classical physics occurs in an old-fashioned house with an elegant billiard room under the staircase and a charming master-bedroom overhead. Modern physics happens in the same house, whenever the master finds himself tripping on the same faulty stair.

Ancient magical numbers find their counterpart in scientific values that find no explanation except in putative fact. The total energy or number of particles in the universe, for example – if that can be called an example.

The phrase "law and order" is highly misleading - and not just in politics. A truly random sequence would be an infinite one in which every possible combination occurred necessarily.

Our lives are tragicomic because they impose the most relentless system on the most anecdotal facts.

La Rochefoucauld skillfully evaded a thicket called self-interest only to find himself lost in a forest called *amour-propre*. He said he rarely laughed. No wonder!

The Selfish Gene is an absurd title. Scientists' metaphors and jokes are invariably more systematic than their sciences.

The fundamental human motive isn't self-interest, but ecstasy or transport. Consider French women's infatuation with *castrati* in the Enlightenment, or the involuntary urination of girls at Beatles' concerts.

Love is the highest ideal of egalitarianism, but also absolutely anathema to it.

True socialism needs Fourier's *Angelicat*, the socialist substitute for sacred prostitutes.

Democracies, like love affairs, tend to begin with many parties and end with two. But a slim third often keeps effective control.

Un train peut en cacher un autre – to be seen at every level-crossing - is the most erotic maxim of the French railway system.

Equality occurs only one-on-one, and rarely even then.

The opposite of equality is not hierarchy. Equality makes hierarchy necessary.

Pure democracy, as Kant said, would be the most arbitrary form of tyranny.

Arrow's theorem proves that democracy is always liable to produce an arbitrary result. But this is not necessarily anti-democratic.

Affirmative action for short people is as unimaginable as it would be for ugly ones. Real justice is a private matter.

The presidential pardon is the ghost of monarchy.

Louis XIV and President Johnson both gave audiences *en selle*. The President defended this practice on democratic grounds, while the Sun King doubtless felt too superior to his subjects to even give a shit.

Modern democracy arrives with privies and private spaces of the kind introduced by Marie Antoinette, whereas Louis XIV had palaces strewn with excrement. Her execution was linked, as a matter of fact, to her bathroom habits.

The inequality between men and women was only intensified by the early modern democracies. Women had much better property rights in the Middle Ages, and the Church formally required their husbands to pleasure them – not just vice-versa as everyone imagines.

Property is a utopian idea and the antithesis of war. It's a mistake to believe there's no property in paradise.

Sadomasochism flourishes and intensifies in egalitarian societies. One *has* to make a difference.

In trying to abolish artificial inequalities egalitarianism threatens to render the natural ones unbearable.

Calling one's parents by their given names as though they were equals may remind us of cultures in which children ritually insult parents on feast days by doing exactly that. But at least the parents reciprocate by insulting their children!

It is no accident that romance between brother and sister figures so prominently as a model of Enlightenment utopia.

In the Trobriand Islands, incestuous siblings were supposed to kill themselves by jumping from tall palms. Strangely, nothing much happened when sometimes they didn't.

We have forgotten the lesson of Rabelais' Isle of Ennasin, where everyone slept with everyone and all had noses shaped like the Ace of Clubs.

**

Around 1800, children's clothes, themselves a novelty, begin to anticipate adult fashions by a whole generation. This marks the beginning of modern childishness.

Whatever one may think about traditional child marriage, modernity has opened children to a double treatment - at once sentimental and abusive - unprecedented in history.

Freud's explanation of the incest taboo was quite wrong. People who desire to sleep with their parents – consciously or not - are no more typical than Stendhal's charming reminiscences of watching his mother undress.

Most people don't want to sleep with their parents for the same reasons that they find other old people repulsive - and because they know them far too well.

The incest taboo in a nutshell: only fuck those you're allowed to kill.

Theology is usually more correct than psychology. Replacing gods and goddesses by fathers and mothers was a huge step backwards in understanding the mind, let alone the soul.

It's taboo to say – or sometimes even to know - what our taboos are all about.

It's lazy to think that we have been programmed to find excrement repulsive because it may carry disease. Witness animals and young children!

We may find others' farts offensive or comic, but only a seriously mad animal doesn't like its own.

Carnal desire is very often the most spiritual.

Chamfort's Italian proverb claims there's no religion below the waist; but there is always a holy communion going on down there, however black the mass.

Our love of gods has always been best expressed by eating them.

When not eating others, the strong tend to eat themselves.

The best argument for meat-eating is that millions of animals would never have existed without it. We don't think humans should never have lived just because they get killed in the end.

Food and drink are a perfect dream for snobs. Democratic television is stuffed with celebrity chefs.

Kissing lies halfway between eating and singing.

Almost all the original taboos were organized around food. Aboriginal tribes permitted public copulation but not public mastication. My own parents found eating in the street more offensive than public kissing.

The mouth makes the ever-concealed anus look clean. No wonder Thackeray began his *Book of Snobs* with a description of eating.

Waning lovers stop kissing long before they stop anything else.

We like white teeth, however false; but ancient peoples blacken theirs - a substitute for knocking them out.

Wittgenstein said that ethics and aesthetics are one and the same - a maxim harder to disprove than one might think right.

Kissing was rare among hunter-gatherers, and there wasn't even a word for it in Japanese until quite recently. Neither philosophy nor science have a decent theory - or even history - of the kiss.

Young women will sometimes kiss but not copulate. Prostitutes quite the reverse.

Feminists who celebrate the archaic primacy of feminine deities may possibly be right about the primacy. But to become a god is the ultimate form of misfortune.

Sexual politics are an acrimonious marriage of church and state with absolutely no hope of divorce.

La Rochefoucauld considered erotic love and ambition mutually exclusive, like love and avarice according to Andreas Capellanus - all the more striking in that neither of them had much good to say about it. Others have compared incest to miserliness.

One cannot speak of tact, let alone provide a theory of it, without being tactless.

It is impossible to make a consistent system out of good manners. Such a system would void them.

It's not that Americans lack politeness; they just don't have an Idea of it. Parisian waiters on the other hand...

Strange to say, the apex of a woman's legs is the vanishing point of Western history.

In the history of painting, Courbet's *L'Origine du monde* gives way to Magritte's *La Représentation*. In neither case can we see the woman's face; but in the latter we can't even see her vagina.

There are many accounts of North African women throwing their skirts over their heads rather than reveal their faces. They're more logical than the rest of us.

Genitals are allegories of the face.

Making a metaphor of blushing, Shakespeare wrote that beauty is always printed in blood. Both the blood and the printing are essential, like the red dots between Hindu women's eyes.

We may complain that classical art too often represents a woman looking at her face in the mirror. But when the mirror shatters, around 1914, we cease to be able to see her at all. Gender collapses into an abstraction called sex.

Sex attracts and repels by virtue of the same powers and dispositions. To be disgusted by pornography is very different from being immune to it.

Sex is a bore. *Capisci*?

Most waking people require physical stimulation to achieve orgasm. But when men and women have wet dreams, they're like Lewis Carroll's White Queen who bleeds before she's been pricked.

I've learned what little I know about sex from women. My polite masseuse and her husband used to take a taxi to swap partners once a month in Rouen, where she told me she liked best to be "taken hard, fast, and from behind." I also attended a lesbian conference in Avignon, not far from the papal palace, at which a speaker was asked about the difference between vaginal and anal sex: "*Eh bien*, it's evidently the same general idea," she replied, "that becomes narrower and more exact when a woman makes her anus for you what her vagina is for others."

The female anus is an artistic topic inasmuch as it is supplemental and fundamental at one and the same time.

The male one is usually just the butt of jokes.

Eros triumphs by transubstantiating disgust. This alone makes it seem like the promised land.

It is no easier to mimic genuine passion than it is for a musician or tennis player to pretend to play well.

Far from illustrating the union of the good and the beautiful rightly advocated by feminists, modern women have often advertised and even exaggerated the perversity of their desires. There's a rather silly story by Anaïs Nin in which a woman recounts being sodomized while watching an execution; and to put the icing on the cake, her diaries say that her father was her best lover.

We should of course feel sorry for people who fall in love only with children. Lewis Carroll is a good example because Alice and the other girls considered him beyond reproach, although he had photographed some of them naked. But how judge those who bed Asians because they look to them so much like children? Or women, like a friend of mine, who like only tall men, and reject all the rest as though they were dwarfs?

Balthus is often anathematized for his depiction of young girls despite or because of his claim that he was painting the sacred. But even Balthus suppressed *The Guitar Lesson* - presumably on musical grounds.

We vilify pedophilia while calling our lovers "babe" and indulging in amorous babytalk. Joyce exploits this rather childishly in *Ulysses*.

Love-making is like a joke: it's flirtation with a punch line.

Women are proverbially attracted to what the English call a good laugh even more than to good looks. A survey in the 1980s found that a majority of Parisian women fantasized about bedding Woody Allen more than any other celebrity in the world. It's hardly surprising, then, that his ex-girlfriend's daughter eventually joined the club.

The most endearing thing about our President is that he married his teacher at the Lycée, twenty-five years his senior, and that their relation began as a crime. It makes one almost proud to be French.

The modern attempt to quarantine sex from power should end by forbidding, not just the young to love the old, but the intelligent to love the stupid, or the beautiful to love the ugly. Indeed, it should forbid falling in love altogether, since there is no greater or more unjust power in the world.

It is often said that spiritual wisdom is accompanied by a sense of humor. The Dalai Lama has described himself as a professional joker, and presumably to prove it, pretended to raise one of his cheeks to fart during an ecumenical meeting – a spiritual exercise duly imitated here.

Thinking sometimes requires laughing if it is not to commit suicide. But laughing itself is often a sort of symbolic suicide - when it isn't actual murder.

When Juliet stabs herself to death - exclaiming "O happy dagger, this is thy sheath!" – she's a hairsbreadth from obscene comedy. *Romeo and Juliet* is really *Pyramus and Thisbe* in which Thisbe is deflowered, not killed, and the lion who eats her is really a man.

***

Men and women are like mirror images: no rotation in Euclidean space can ever make them coincide.

That transexuals are frequently called "non-binary" beggars belief.

In initiation rites, girls become boys for a period and vice-versa. To become one, you must know as intimately as possible what it is like to be the other. There's always an imaginary copula.

Until the fifteenth century English children were called girls, girls were called gay girls, and servants were called boys. Meanwhile boys were dressed as girls in the nineteenth-century, and blue was a girl's color until the 1920s, while nothing was more virile than pink. All clear?

The hygiene of heterosexuality lies in its idealization and exaggeration of natural differences. Other forms tend to exaggerate the exaggerations.

Yuval Harari's explanation for male dominance sounds like Aristophanes' jokes about the political skills of gay men.

Eight percent of sheep are supposed to be "gay," i.e., to sodomize other sheep. I'm surprised it's not more, since they're such great imitators – like my friends in the theatre.

There is an ancient Greek adage that the most attractive males have the same *eidos* or form as females, and vice-versa. Even Lolita has a boy's knees.

Wounds on young men were considered by the Greeks to enhance their beauty, while those on the old were regarded as shameful. Only in modernity did women come to be called the fair sex - as though their orifices were wounds.

Feminists rightly make a link between the idolization of female beauty and the victimization of women. Certain sorts of victim have always been idolized.

It's impossible to imagine Chaucer, or Boccaccio, or even Chrétien de Troyes writing Poe's line that there's no more poetical subject than the death of a beautiful woman.

The strong are maximally attractive only if they're vulnerable. Women and ancient Greeks conventionally fall for soldiers, but above all for wounded ones.

During the Second World War some women thought it their duty to pleasure the soldiers who were sacrificing their lives for them. While this was also an excuse to be pleasured themselves, the element of self-sacrifice was quite genuine and - as my mother observed at the time – doubtless no small part of the pleasure.

I once bet – like an inveterate loser - with a young woman who seemed to be implacably lesbian, as she had never been remotely attracted to a male in her entire life. Ten years later she invited me out to dinner with her new husband - and I thought what a pity! Of course, homosexual relations are a traditional preparation for marriage, but I had much preferred her old boyish girlfriend to the new dandy.

A study of fashion might be forgiven for concluding that Socrates was quite serious to assert that the difference between men and women consists essentially in their hair-length.

A man without a beard is like a woman with a beard. (Chekhov)

Fashionable young men currently wear trousers so baggy that they appear to have no buttocks. They're the opposite of classical ballet dancers and American footballers whose bums are so ostentatiously outlined, just like contemporary women in tights.

Women wear hose, as men did in the Renaissance, to idealize their legs. But filming them naked has comparable effects.

Miniskirts and tights were long ago made fashionable by Renaissance men. This was the origin of the codpiece as tunics rose ever higher up the thighs.

Should there now be an equivalent for women? Or will nothing suffice?

I heard a woman say at a party: "This skirt is a bit impractical on circular stairs. Everyone can see what I had for dinner."

Karl Krauss' sexist maxim that women who are never ugly are never beautiful can just as well be applied to women's tastes in men and their penises.

The limp penis is an old model of the joke, but Dionysiac rites the world over prove that the erect one was even more hysterical.

The phallus lies at the origins of comedy, and reigns only in ritual and myth.

Presumably speaking from experience, Tiresias claimed that female sexual pleasure is keener than the male. Sade predictably agreed that to be penetrated is more exquisite than merely to be its instrument. But insofar as the latter joy mainly consists of imagining the former, it's doubtless really a matter of how far the body defers to the soul.

With typical French honesty, we call sadism *le vice Anglais*. But on this side of the English Channel we have not only Sade himself and Anne Desclos, but also Robbe-Grillet and Michel Foucault. It says everything about the structure of sadism that the novelist's wife was his bottom – but after his death became a top for everyone else.

If you want to imagine what Shakespeare thought about sex, consider his portrayal of Achilles as sodomizing an older man while at the same time being in love with Hector's sister. Someone says that he'd be better off throwing Hector to the ground than downing his sister, but instead Achilles develops a longing to be sodomized by the very same man that later he will murder in cold blood. Meanwhile, Ajax runs around the battlefield *looking for himself*: a jakes, or what the Americans call a John.

Contemporary sex experts seem unable to grasp why some shamans enjoy sex with both men and women, but not with each other. It's no use calling them "bisexual" or "queer."

The Spanish husband of a friend of mine used to wolf-whistle and solicit tourists on the backstreets of Toledo. When we accused him of *machismo,* he responded that about one in thirty women acquiesced – and perhaps surprisingly, the pretty more often than the plain.

Kleptomania has been classified as a sexual perversion, and the great majority of kleptomaniacs are female as compared with fetishists who are usually male. It might be objected that kleptomaniacs fetishize money and possessions; but they are really in love with the act of theft itself. A famous American actress stole from a shop she could easily have bought, and the kleptomaniacs I have known have all been rich.

The blind are incapable of erotic love, according to Andreas Capellanus, because love is caused by suffering that comes from sight. Far from revealing a shortcoming of the blind, this view is eminently compatible with his Rule XIII: *Amor raro consuevit durare vulgatus* – a maxim better left untranslated.

Both cynics and moralists never tire of repeating that the chase is more exciting than the reward; but the young Queen Victoria refutes them. She had two keyholes in her bedroom door so the servants couldn't enter while she was fucking Albert – a thing she never tired of. And yet we call the Victorian age the age of prudery!

Sylvia Plath's famous line that every woman loves a fascist is certainly striking, coming as it does from a very intelligent woman. But even gorillas do not always fancy the most dominant male. Faced, so to speak, with a confused virgin, they will sometimes reach back to guide his penis gently with their hands.

"When you go to see a woman, don't forget your whip" – a maxim attributed by Nietzsche to an old woman – is usually suppressed by his modern admirers. They prefer the more edifying anecdote that he went mad after seeing a horse – an ass in one account – whipped in Turin. But the one hardly contradicts the other.

The truth is that most of us are indifferent to others' love unless we need them, or unless it comes in the form of group adulation.

The time taken for love to be reduced to indifference reflects not so much the quality of the love as the intensity of the indifference.

True betrayal lies in the hairsbreadth between carelessness and passion.

**

In word though not indeed, violence is its own cure, like poetry.

Beauty is not something given, but a promise that may or may not be kept.

Prediction is very difficult, especially of the future.

Originality does not consist in creating something new - which happens every day - but in rediscovering the origins. This is the point of Borges' story about a man who attempts to rewrite *Don Quixote* word for word: i.e., to predict the past.

What is said only once cannot be heard; what is said more than once cannot be true.

A certain sort of poetry - like Cioran's - is destined to be a failed allegory of universal failure.

Poetry – not just the detective story - is a kind of cult of the kill.

A poem is not a psychological experiment any more than a mathematical proof is a scientific one.

Through the Looking-Glass is a masterpiece of children's logic that few adults seem to understand. Someone must surely have figured out by now that Alice's cat is called Dinah because all the poetry is about fish. But no one has ever explained why the trees are full of eggs instead of apples. It's because of what happens at the end of every chess game.

An artist's logic: to depict you faithfully I must conceal you and portray everything else around that void.

Art is not a remedy for catastrophe; it often causes it.

It is said that the inability to be an artist makes a critic, but the reverse is more common.

Contemporary artists are called *cutting-edge* because they exploit the ugly, authentic because they parody the real, socially conscious because they're shamelessly didactic, and, to add insult to injury, often become obscenely rich by idealizing the poor.

We are so keen to put tragedy to use, and even find redemption in it, because tragedy is so utterly pointless.

Pitch black has a wavelength of nil. It is more coherent than "white" light - which, as everyone knows, is a hodgepodge.

We still don't know how cats purr, but I know why. It's like laughing, only better. They do it when happy and when frightened. In fact, the first purr in history doubtless occurred when a very nice kitten had just had a very nasty scare – just like Isaac in *Genesis*.

Big cats can roar but not purr. They don't need to; but from this strength they derive a weakness.

It's dangerous to have any organ that's too strong in case it overwhelms the others.

Since absolutely nothing fundamental can be known, and what is most important can't be taught, the best teachers are always to some degree inscrutable, like the face of a mountain, or *Madame Bovary*.

The true way is to fall off the tightrope while imitating a drunk; the false way is to claim to have mastered it sober.

Compared to love, however hopeless, friendship is like that kind of madness which holds a conversation with the furniture.
.

The First World War was the last archaic one. The enemies played football together at Christmas.

British soldiers in the Second World War at first tended to fire away from the enemy. Horrified, their commanders replaced abstract targets by straw men – a strategy that never fails.

Human flesh tastes like pork, so little wonder that Plato's brother's vegetarian city was called the City of Pigs – an impossible city far preferable to the ridiculous one proposed by Socrates.

Leo Strauss tried to teach philosophers to read. But they still don't understand why *The Republic* takes place in a democracy with slaves, and why it begins with Socrates being compelled to have the whole discussion in the first place.

It is sometimes better not to see the wood for the trees.

To be seduced by words and images is an advantage for the average writer and may even produce a very good one. For these, however, it is also a grave temptation – like *Finnegans Wake*.

"Moderation in all things, above all moderation," is a maxim attributed to Oscar Wilde; but it's really Plato's reply to Aristotle.

Not to believe in free will means nothing because one can't do otherwise. But everybody acts as though they believed in it, and the second funniest solution to the paradox of freedom argues from this compulsion.

Proust conceived of us not as animals, but like plants that mimic animals. If the body grows willy-nilly, why not the soul?

Freedom is never possible, for if it's possible it must be necessary.

Dogmatists? Despise them. Why? No one knows. (Flaubert)
.

We fancy ourselves immortal to flatter beliefs that make sense only because we aren't.

It would insult Saint Augustine to call him the Christian Hawking, although he too insisted that the world was created not in five days, as I'd always thought, but an instantaneous Big Bang. Professor Hawking ridiculed those who asked what came before, but his more congenial collaborator Penrose now says such Bangs may be serial. Hell!

Hell would be an eternal poetry reading, or, even worse, excerpts from a novel.

"Nothing is impossible to imagine" is merely an advertising slogan. But it's impossible to imagine nothing.

Maxims are perfect for lazy people. Fifty years ago everyone in France was proclaiming that the novel was dead; but since then novels seem to be getting longer and longer, and to little avail.

Bataille thought *Wuthering Heights* one of the great books about evil. Like everyone else, however, he failed to identify its four hundred and ninety-first sin – the unforgivable one - which lies not in desiring to excess, hanging puppies, or marrying for revenge, but in losing all interest in someone as soon as they reciprocate. This happens, I'm sorry to say, as early as page 5 in my edition.

We are great because only we know how small we are.

The houses in my town were all black when I was young. Since they have been whitewashed, nostalgia makes them blacker than ever.

Sartre claimed that all intelligent people are kind. If you disagree, you must be like that fool Newton - or a believer in *amathia*.

Pain is the last metaphysical marker.

.

One of the least mentioned joys of having our loves requited is that we are suddenly free to think of something else.

We tend to conceive power as the subjugation of the weak by the strong. But sadists soon discover who's really in charge, and the most ancient kings gained their power, like martyrs, from being sacrificed.

The modern dogma that desire and gender are independent variables is either in bad faith or delirious.

Just as people mistake unfamiliar music for noise, we still mistake a complicated system for no system at all.

Some people are lucky that their limitations happen to coincide with the world's.

Capuchin monkeys bang mussels against trees, not to break their shells as we might, but to tire their muscles until they open of their own accord. *Ars longa, vita brevis.*

Scarecrows notwithstanding, animals are not usually fooled by puppets; they generally ignore or attack them.

It is the fate of many genuine originals to appear reactionary, and all phony ones to be it.

Except in emergencies, we must be atheists in politics. Parties make the old gods look almost dignified. Simone Weil said they should be abolished.

Keynes thought sex and drugs much more important than economics, which he compared to dentistry. But he also classed speculation as an addiction that no medicine could cure.

Not to enter the lottery is irrational, since it makes impossible what would otherwise just be unlikely. But many prefer to sacrifice everything rather than risk losing a little bit.

Happiness is finally impossible for most of us. For either we're glad to go - in which case life must have become burdensome - or we're not. The *happy few* are those enchanting creatures who positively desire to die.

Most people die just because they can't help it. (Chögyam Trungpa)

We tend to think those we have loved more unhinged than they really are, for it would be humiliating if they had betrayed us out of mere indifference.

The best fiction is not disguised autobiography but the thing itself.

What can the heart teach us except to value disappointment?

To get a sense of the deeper side of the even numbers, consider evening and twilight, and even the grammar of this sentence.

Twins and evens have always been a cause for alarm. Lolita first sleeps with Humbert Humbert in Room 342, a room full of mirrors.

The unrepeatable is just what is repeated, in history as in the bedroom.

Mathematics is an ideal introduction to poetry. Poetry is an introduction to nothing. It's the end.

The blue sky, children's laughter, an array of deadly weapons.

***

Euler's identity is a box with a transcendental lock that can only be opened with an imaginary key.

Flaubert noted that architects always forget to put in the stairs. This distinguishes them from mere builders.

The contours of happiness are necessarily those of the landscape in which one happens to live. Unhappiness always lives elsewhere.

A value might be regarded as a theory of the facts that cannot be proved or falsified, though it must be right or wrong.

If everyone spoke truthfully it would poison intercourse beyond repair.

Even Aristotle, who famously defended poetry as a science of the possible, conceded that the highest sort of poetry is impossible.

Christians used to prosecute animals and even provide them with lawyers. But now we call ourselves animals, only we can be prosecuted.

Since atheists deny not just all previous gods but all future ones, they can have little conception of what infant divinities they're denying. Little Whiteheads perhaps?

The well-tempered clavier is slightly out of tune, like conventional wisdom. True wisdom has wolf-notes.

Pythagoras' comma is the happy fall.

Solution means dissolving, so solutions are sometimes desirable and sometimes not.

A function may endlessly approach a value without reaching it, but the transcendental numbers have no value to reach. They're liquidity itself [*elle-même*].

All the fundamental paradoxes concern the continuum: point and line, particle and wave, digital and analog, algebra and geometry, the individual and the group. We've solved none of them.

Pessimism is the only possible philosophy, but that doesn't mean it's true. No true philosophy is complete. So only an incomplete pessimism might not be false.

In the course of a lifetime most people are accused of a multitude of crimes – often all except those that they have committed.

Even if it were possible to suspend judgment about the most important things, we would still be forced to act as though we hadn't.

Unless time can run backwards, every genuine development is a form of transcendence. Children – to spite philosophers - manage it all the time.

Happiness, like the sky, is just as far away as it appears to be.